2

#	TEAM	PLAYER	PAGE
1	SAINT LOUIS CARDINALS	YADIER MOLINA	9
2	MILWAUKEE BREWERS	CHRISTIAN YELICH	11
3	CHICAGO CUBS	KYLE HENDRICKS	13
4	CINCINNATI REDS	JOEY VOTTO	15
5	PITTSBURGH PIRATES	KE BRYAN HAYES	17
6	ATLANTA BRAVES	RONALD ACUÑA	19
7	WASHINTONG NATIONALS	JUAN SOTO	21
8	NEW YORK METS	PETE ALONSO	23
9	PHILLADELPHIA PHILLIES	BRYCE HARPER	25
10	MIAMI MARLINS	SANDY ALCÁNTARA	27
11	LOS ANGELES DODGERS	MOOKIE BETTS	29
12	ARIZONA DBACKS	KETEL MARTE	31
13	SAN FRANCISCO GIANTS	BRANDON BELT	33
14	COLORADO ROKIES	KRIS BRYANT	35
15	SAN DIEGO PADRES	FERNANDO TATIS	37
16	NEW YORK YANKEES	AARON JUDGE	41
17	TAMPA BAY RAYS	RANDY AROZARENA	43
18	BOSTON RED SOX	XANDER BOGAERTS	45
19	TORONTO BLUE JAYS	VLADIMIR GUERRERO JR	47
20	BALTIMORE ORIOLES	JOHN MEANS	49
21	MINNESOTA TWINS	BYRON BUXTON	51
22	CLEVELAND INDIANS	SHANE BIEBER	53
23	CHICAGO WHITE SOX	TIM ANDERSON	55
24	KANSAS CITY ROYALS	SALVADOR PÉREZ	57
25	DETROIT TIGERS	AKIL BADDOO	59
26	HOUSTON ASTROS	ALEX BREGMAN	61
27	OACKLAND ATHLETICS	RAMÓN LAUREANO	63
28	TEXAS RANGERS	COREY SEAGER	65
29	LOS ANGELES ANGELS	MIKE TROUT	67
30	SEATTLE MARINERS	JULIO RODRÍGUEZ	69

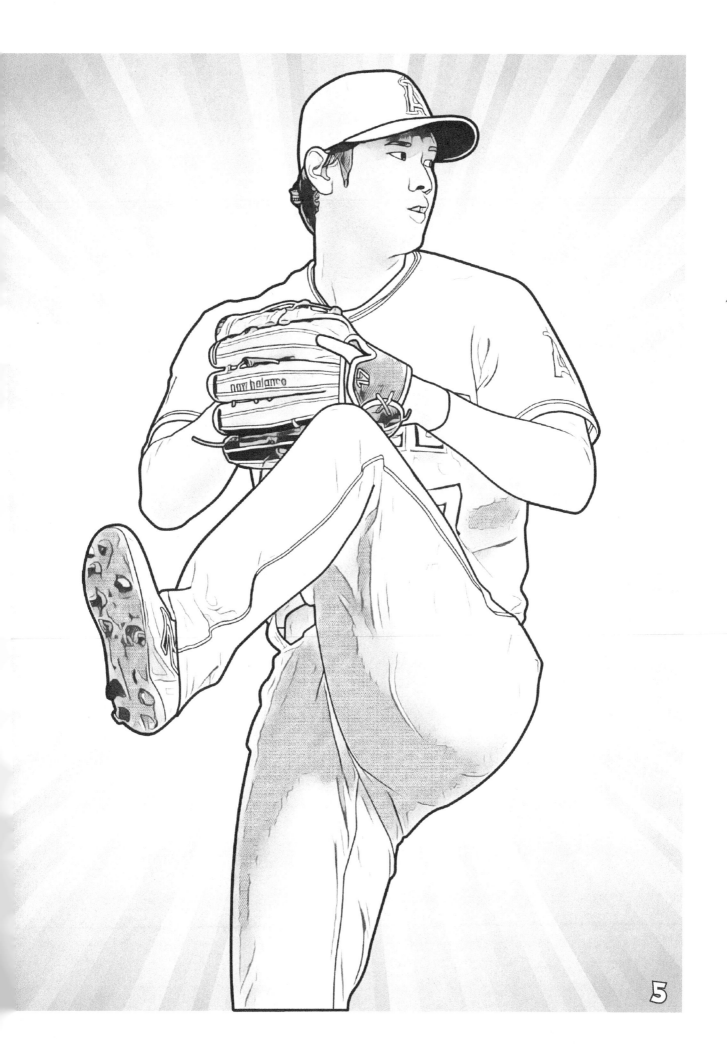

6

NATIONAL LEAGUE

12

16

18

19

23

26

33

35

36

38

AMERICAN LEAGUE

41

43

47

50

51

60

63

64

68

69

I hope you enjoyed the book.
If you liked it, leave us a nice review on
Amazon and your comments so we can keep
improving!

We really appreciate your suggestions
and we will be happy to implement your
recommendations.

14280572R00044